Start TO Finish
Second Series

FROM Spore TO Mushroom

LISA OWINGS

LERNER PUBLICATIONS Minneapolis

Lerner Publications Company
A division of Lerner Publishing Group, Inc.
241 First Avenue North
Minneapolis, MN 55401 USA

For reading levels and more information, look up this title at www.lernerbooks.com.

Library of Congress Cataloging-in-Publication Data

Names: Owings, Lisa, author.
Title: From spore to mushroom / Lisa Owings.
Other titles: Start to finish (Minneapolis, Minn.).
    Second series.
Description: Minneapolis : Lerner Publications, 2017.
    | Series: Start to finish. Second series | Includes
    bibliographical references and index.
Identifiers: LCCN 2016037258 (print) | LCCN
    2016038337 (ebook) | ISBN 9781512434415
    (lb : alk. paper) | ISBN 9781512450934 (eb pdf)
Subjects: LCSH: Mushrooms—Life cycles—Juvenile
    literature.
Classification: LCC QK617 .O86 2017 (print) | LCC
    QK617 (ebook) | DDC 579.6—dc23

LC record available at https://lccn.loc.gov/2016037258

Manufactured in the United States of America
1-42090-25384-9/27/2016

TABLE OF Contents

Look at these mushrooms! How do they grow?

First, a mushroom releases its spores.

A mushroom spreads its cap. This part of the mushroom looks like an umbrella. Underneath it are soft parts called gills. Between the gills lie millions of spores. They wait to be released. They drift away on the wind.

The spores land and start to grow.

The spores are like seeds. Some land where mushrooms can easily grow. These spores sprout **hyphae**. These are a little like roots.

Then they seek a mate.

The hyphae snake through the soil. Two hyphae from different spores cross paths and join. When this happens, they can make a mushroom.

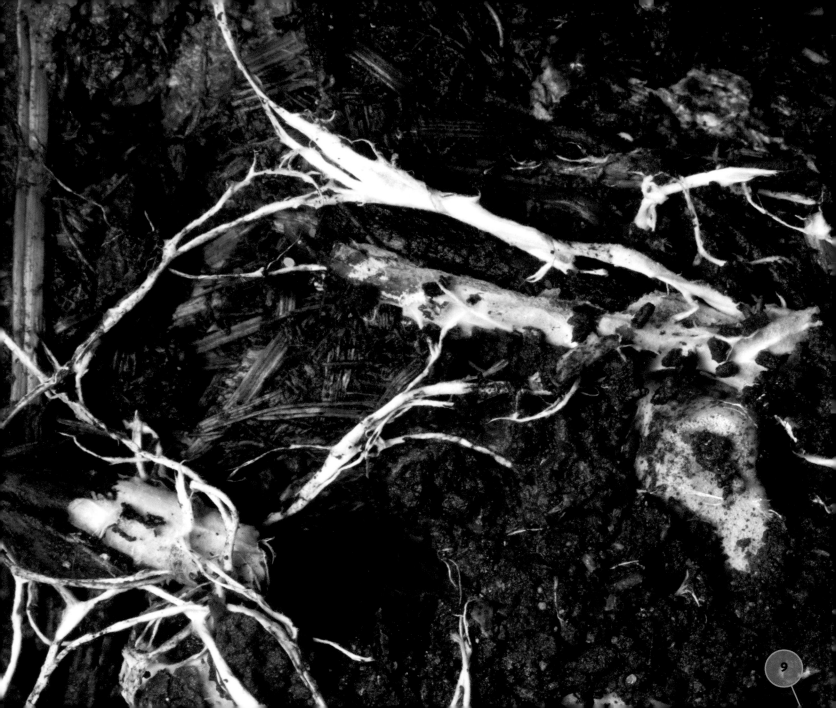

The fungus grows roots.

More hyphae shoot out to support the fungus. The hyphae form a part called the mycelium. It gathers nutrients the fungus needs to grow.

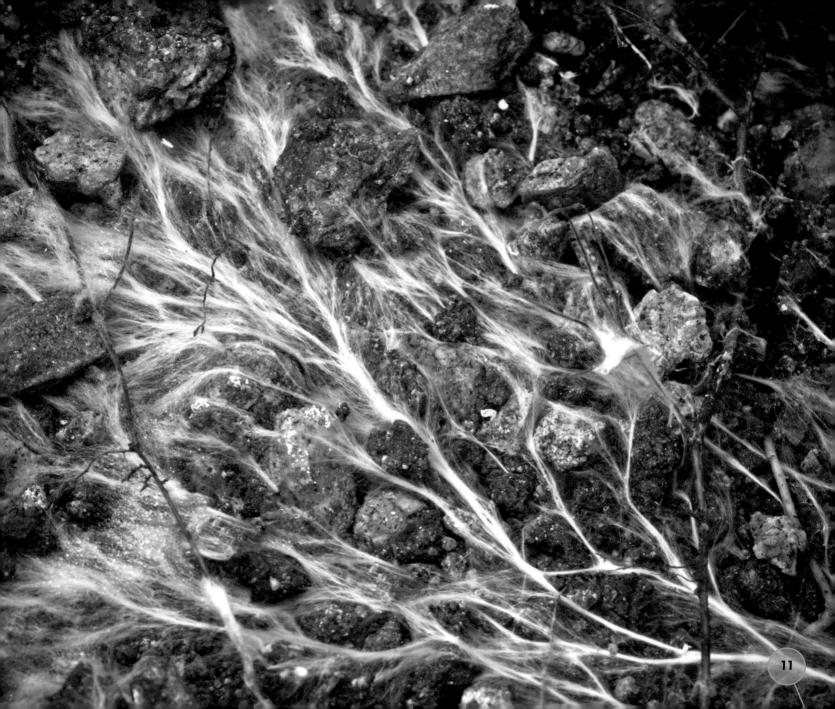

Next, a mushroom bud forms.

The fungus waits until conditions are right.
Then it gets ready to send up its fruit. The
mycelium forms a small bud at the surface of
the soil. This will become the new mushroom.

Soon a baby mushroom appears.

The mushroom bud grows into a small, egg-like ball. It is protected by a soft outer shell called a **veil**. The shell contains a tiny mushroom.

The mushroom breaks through its shell.

The rounded cap of the mushroom breaks through the veil. Pieces of the torn veil can often be seen on the growing mushroom.

The mushroom fruit takes shape.

The mushroom grows larger, and its tightly closed cap reaches outward. Different types of mushrooms develop in different ways. Each has its own unique shape.

The new mushroom continues the cycle!

The new mushroom is fully grown. It releases its spores on the wind. It provides meals for hungry bugs and animals—even humans! Then it **decays**, and new mushrooms sprout in its place.

Glossary

decays: slowly breaks down

fungus: a living thing that often looks like a plant but has no flowers and that lives on dead or decaying things. A mushroom is a fungus.

hyphae: the rootlike threads that make up the mycelium of a fungus

mate: one of a pair of hyphae. Mated hyphae can make a new mushroom.

mycelium: the network of hyphae that forms beneath mushrooms and gathers nutrients

nutrients: substances that plants, animals, and people need to live and grow

spores: cells made by mushrooms and some other plants. Spores are like seeds and can grow new mushrooms.

veil: a covering

Further Information

Boothroyd, Jennifer. *Let's Visit the Deciduous Forest*. Minneapolis: Lerner Publications, 2017. Learn what's in a deciduous forest in this fun walk through a biome.

The Children's University of Manchester
http://www.childrensuniversity.manchester.ac.uk/interactives/science/microorganisms/mushroomlifecycle
Cool animations help you learn more about fungi on this site.

Fleisher, Paul. *Forest Food Webs in Action*. Minneapolis: Lerner Publications, 2014. Find out how mushrooms fit into the forest ecosystem.

Microbe Magic
http://microbemagic.ucc.ie/about_microbes/fungi.html
Learn the good, the bad, and the ugly about microbes.

USDA: Mind-Boggling Facts about Mushrooms
https://www.ars.usda.gov/oc/kids/farm/story4/mushroomfacts
Check out these fun facts about mushrooms!

Index

Photo Acknowledgments
The images in this book are used with the permission of: © iStockphoto.com/Butsaya, p. 1; © Matthijs Wetterauw/Shutterstock, p. 3; © Vaclav Volrab/Shutterstock.com, p. 5; © Ciabou Hany/Minden Pictures, p. 7; © Nigel Cattlin/Science Source, p. 9; © Emmanuel LATTES/Alamy, p. 11; © rysp/Bigstock.com, p. 13; © Palana/Bigstock.com, p. 15; © blickwinkel/biopix/Alamy, p. 17; © Elizabeth Pratt/Alamy, p. 19; © BARRI/Shutterstock.com, p. 21.

Cover: © iStockphoto.com/swkunst.

Main body text set in Arta Std Book 20/26.
Typeface provided by International Typeface Corp.